THE TWINS

Verse play

Shakemore Dirani

Mwanaka Media and Publishing Pvt Ltd,
Chitungwiza Zimbabwe
*
Creativity, Wisdom and Beauty

Publisher: *Mmap*
Mwanaka Media and Publishing Pvt Ltd
24 Svosve Road, Zengeza 1
Chitungwiza Zimbabwe
mwanaka@yahoo.com
mwanaka13@gmail.com
www.africanbookscollective.com/publishers/mwanaka-media-and-publishing
https://facebook.com/MwanakaMediaAndPublishing/

Distributed in and outside N. America by African Books Collective
orders@africanbookscollective.com
www.africanbookscollective.com

ISBN: 978-1-77934-042-9
EAN: 9781779340429

© Shakemore Dirani 2024

All rights reserved.
No part of this book may be reproduced or transmitted in any form or by any means, mechanical or electronic, including photocopying and recording, or be stored in any information storage or retrieval system, without written permission from the publisher

DISCLAIMER
All views expressed in this publication are those of the author and do not necessarily reflect the views of *Mmap*.

Acknowledgements.

The author would like to thank the following people: Mai Chipidza of Morgan Zintec who patiently read through some of my writings and encouraged me to continue writing; Mr George Mujajati of Morgan Zintec who read through this manuscript and gave me invaluable advice on writing and Mr Missy Hammad my brother and friend who helped me with the initial typing and other technical aspects.

DEDICATED

To my father, the late Mr Jorum Dirani, who always wanted to publish a book but never did, but all the same inspired me with his writings.

The Twins *is a purely fictional work. Although the idea was conceived from the great Zimbabwean crisis of 2008 it is an epic story that will find timeless parallels in all situations where power is being contested. All the characters are the creation of the writer, any resemblance to any living person is coincidental and unintended.*

"…love cools, friendship falls off,
Brothers divide:
In cities, mutinies; in countries, discord;
In palaces, treason;
And the bond cracked 'twixt son and father."

William Shakespeare in King Lear.

Dramatis Personae

Chibwe the King

Hunter and Farmer - *twin sons of the king*

Mazwi-the-Poet

The Teacher aka Blue Necktie

School Children —Promise

-Clever

-Future

Old Man

Old Woman

Preacher

Preacher's Disciple 1

Preacher's Disciple 2

Soldier 1

Soldier 2

Foreigners -Ally

-Consultant

ACT ONE SCENE 1

In the tower of mysteries also known as Dzimbahwe an aging but still healthy king is wearing his full regalia sitting in his royal chair. The king's chamber has two entrances: on the right and on the left. At each door is a soldier standing at full attention. For a long time, king Chibwe has been engrossed in deep thought, now he seems to have reached a decision.

KING:

(Calling) Hunter! Farmer! Come here right now!
(Two identical young men of about thirty enter into palace, one is holding a hoe the other, a bow and some arrows. They kneel down in gesture of respect)
Hunter, take the seat to my right.
Farmer, to my left sit,
Leave your gumboots outside the door.
(The Twins comply and take seats)
Listen very carefully to what I'm going to say.

HUNTER:

O Great King I am listening.
(Aside) Some good news, I hope, for the slayer of lions.

FARMER:

Thank you Munhumutapa I am listening
(Aside) My ears have been tickling since yesterday,
Surely today I shall hear things that make me smile.

KING:

Just like yesterday I was the prince,
Fluttering with youth like a flower in the morning.

Now the hours have sapped my power
And looking back I see I was just a leaf
That weathered a season on the tree of life.
Now that leaf is yellowed; the writing is on the wall.

HUNTER and FARMER:
(shift in their seats glancing around, together)
Where! Where!

KING:
Ignoring their interjections, scans the two faces before him)
Every good leader must know when it's time to say good bye,
Lest he begins to punish the prophets and reward the flatterers,
My father, that old sage, used to say.
I realize that the state has gone full circle
And it's my turn to relinquish the crown, usher in the next ruler.

FARMER:
(Jerking to his feet) O thank you father,
Here I am ready and waiting!

HUNTER:
(Dashing forward) Phew! There is a time for everything,
Who can deny Hunter his well-deserved Crown?

KING:

Sit down. *(the twins sit)*
Your reactions spell out my crisis.
I am a lucky king blessed with two first-borns,
But the symbols of my pride are the sources of my dilemma.
My sleep is troubled at night when I go to bed,
To which one of you should I hand the Crown
Both of you being equal in my heart?

HUNTER:
To me, of- course.
When the lion is roaring outside in the evening
Who is it that ventures into the night to drive the terror away?

FARMER:
Give The Crown to Farmer who stays at home
Receiving delegates and dignitaries of state
While this stranger to the state
Wanders across jungles trailing the scent of apes.
Who wants a ruler who stays in the bush?

HUNTER:
You stay in the kitchen because of your cowardice.
A man who fears even a frog!
Who doesn't know your…?

KING:
Patience. Be patient.
It is not the past that I am thinking of but the future

You have all done well in the past,
But I seek one who will do well going forwards.
How can I elect one without offending the other?
I fear to offend Farmer,
Who has strived to put a plate of maize meal before me
Ever since he learnt to walk.
And I fear to disappoint my daring Hunter
Who must snatch prey from the claws of beasts
To garland my dinner-table with steak.
(He rises to his feet and paces about the room)
Those are my fears, my children,
But if it will be you, Farmer to rule,
Take tender care of my people
As you would your calves and cauliflowers…

FARMER:
You worry yourself needlessly, father,
I will make a paradise of this country,
The place where even rivers sing hymns
While …

KING:
If it will be you Hunter, upon the throne
Use the strength of your arm and mind
To guard my people against jackal and hyena.

HUNTER:
That is not a problem to me, father;
I will rule this land so splendidly

That the Great Munhumutapa will smile in his grave.

KING:
I'm not worried about what you will do with The Crown;
I know you have plenty of such grandiose schemes,
I'm worried about what you will do if you *do not* get the crown.
How will you take it if the crown goes to your brother and not to you?
I want to hear your views on that one.
Speak, Farmer, my wise first born –
Respecting our Shona belief that says the twin born last is the elder.

Loud singing interrupts the proceedings. From the right enter a sixtish old man clad in a garish red suit, purple shirt and yellow shoes. his name is Mazwi-the-Poet.

MAZWI:
(Singing and gesturing)
Good morning Zimbabwe-ants
Black-ants, white-ants and flying-ants
If all you ants put your ant-ics together
What a great ant-hill you'd build!
But if you choose to be milit-ant
And indign-ant like tyr-ants
Then the Tower of Dzimbahwe
Will not differ from Babel.

FARMER:

Excuse us, Old Fellow; this is not a time for jokes.

MAZWI:
Some of the farmers in our local paradise
Have just invented a remote-controlled hoe.
Some of the hunters have lost their scent
And now want to hunt between street and avenue...

KING:
You are right, *Sahwira*; but do leave us for now.

FARMER:
Soldier, take that rambler away.

THE SOLDIER FROG-MARCHES HIM OUT. AS HE IS THROWN OUT THE POET'S VOICE ECHOES BACK.

POET'S VOICE:
Farmer, you are not the king already,
More-over this year you harvested more black-jack
Than your barley and beans combined... (*Voice fades*)

FARMER:
(*Clicking his tongue irritably*) Tsk! It's a bad omen
To meet a mad-man first thing in the morning.

HUNTER:
Are you still scolding the poet?

Father, hear what I have always said,
He uses his forked tongue again!

KING:
You empty gourds with tongues for food
And none for good words!
Your tongues shall plant fire and shoot arrows!
Speak, Farmer!

FARMER:
(*Rising and saluting*) *Ahoy* Dzimbahwe!
Ahoy, Great Heart!
Let me rule and you will not regret…

KING:
Thanks for the slogans
But give us your best ideas first.

HUNTER:
Hear him! The barbed tongue is at it again!
Ask him to pray for supper
And he puts in it a parable of propaganda!

KING:
Let not the millipede mock the snail's speed,
You are no better yourself!
Speak Farmer.

FARMER:

Thank you, O Great Sage,
Great son of Chaminuka,
The one steady as the balancing rocks of Epworth...!

KING:
Yes, I am Chaminuka's grandson,
But I shall soon stop you if all you have are slogans.

FARMER:
In floods, in drought or in rains fair,
Who is it that keeps widow and orphan alive?
If by your word or by a freak chance I am not chosen
Then just give me my inheritance in the form of a hoe
And an acre of land beside a river,
There to continue with my green business
While my brother sits in the magnificent Tower
Ruling states as did the Great Munhumutapa.
(He sits)

KING:
Thank you, but next time put your ideas into fewer words.
Hunter, you can speak.

: HUNTER
(Standing up and bowing) Thank you for according me this honour, O
Great Inyangani, the everlasting rock.
Sociologically, this forthcoming paradigm shift
Requires ethno-methodology to counteract the detrimental effects
of obliquity, and the metamorphosis henceforth...

KING:
Mai we-e-e! Mai we, mai —we!
I could have been impressed if your big education had taught you the wisdom to carry with you a good dictionary.

HUNTER:
I was simply saying that....
(Poet re-enters from the left, interrupts him)

MAZWI:
Never trust anyone who says, I was *thimbly thaying*;
(To the king) Sahwira, a lil'whiff of power in the wind
And your children catch of it like starved hyenas.

FARMER:
O father, why do you tolerate this lunatic?

KING:
And you, why do you tolerate the beard on your face?
(A soldier pushes the poet out of the room)
Soldier, *never* do anything to that fellow except on my orders.
(Soldier salutes)
Speak, Hunter!

HUNTER:
The lion hides when he sees me
For the jaws of many a lion I have torn
I am a well-travelled man; I have seen and learned

Many good things abroad that can improve us here.
(*Beating his chest*) Even my brother here
Knows that I am a man of hard steel;
Metal which eats other metals.

KING:
Instead of metal I prefer you boast of *mettle*.

HUNTER:
I was simply saying that if I fail to make it to the throne,
Then I shall be content to take my bow
And go back to shooting warthog
Leaving my brother to rule in peace.

KING:
Alright, thank you my sons, for your promises,
I trust you have the integrity to keep them.
On the twenty-seventh of June
I shall hand over the crown to one of you.
How will I choose my successor?
Maybe I will just toss a coin
And let blind-fate be my advisor.
Probably I will ask the people through a vote
And elect the person of their choice.
Perhaps I will take the third route
Which you know nothing of now.
Whatever the case, here's a word of advice;
Hold your tongues, my children.
Talk to the old folks with respect

Teach the young ones wisely,
And be gentle even with tramps
Who will come just to shake your palace gates.
For by the testimony of all these people
Will my hand surely be swayed
When the twenty-seventh comes.
You can go now.
(EXEUNT ALL)

ACT ONE: SCENE 2

On the road enter Farmer, he is alone. He gestures to himself apparently in deep thought. On one side of the stage there is a congregation and a preacher but Farmer does not see them at first. He is talking to himself as he walks.

FARMER:
Teach to the young ones wisely,
Talk to the old folks with respect, the King said.
That means he is going to use the people's opinion to choose the next king.
(*He sees the preacher and stands a-distant listening to his words*)

PREACHER:
(*in a loud voice*) We are a chosen people
But our way of living must make it clear to the world
Whether we are a chosen of the ever living God
Or a chosen of the undying Satan.
Hallelujah!

PEOPLE:
(*together*) *Ame-em!*

PREACHER:
Samson met his demise through dear Delilah-
So my good brothers and sisters, remember this
Every devil comes clothed in a terrible beauty
But from every devil there is a way to salvation:

Therefore, fast and pray the angels of our Lord
Will lead us to the Promised Land.

FARMER:
(*Approaching slowly, talking to himself*)
What! All those people listening to one person!
Let me ask him for a favour
To sow a few pumpkin seeds among his sunflowers.
Hope Hunter has not poisoned them already.
(*Aloud to the Preacher*)
Peace be unto you good shepherd!

PREACHER:
Peace!

FARMER:
I can see your flock is fine and well-fed;
Verily I say to you, if things work our way, before June is out
You shall be minister of a higher anointing
So that the entire flock of this land
May graze and lie on green pastures too.
Allow me one minute to speak to your flock.

PREACHER:
(*Addressing the congregation*)
When the prince leaves palace to come to church
Expect good things.
I shall not babble in tongues

While my good Lord stands here
Bubbling with a greater promise for us.
Please do lend our Prince sixty seconds of your time.
(The people clap hands, some ululate and whistle).

FARMER:
Thank you. Thank you so much.
I am Boaz the great farmer;
My cattle are as big and as many
As the elephants of Gonarezhou,
My stacks of wheat rise higher than the hills of Vumba.
Some of you have come to glean in my fields
And have not gone hungry.

DISCIPLE 1:
(whispering, to a nearby fellow) His minute is over,
Still I haven't picked the grain of wit in his speech.

DISCIPLE 2:
(Whispering back) Patience is a virtue,
Give him a chance.

FARMER:
But I shall not forget the Almighty who gave me all I have,
Therefore, I bring my ten percent tithe to your church,
Thank you. *(He hands a paper to The Preacher and sits, the people applaud).*

PREACHER:
(Reading cheque) Fifteen Billion dollars!

Raise your hands all ye glad hearts
And lend me your voice in the form of thunder
To thank this blessed servant of God!

THE PEOPLE ARE ELATED, THEY CLAP HANDS, HOOT
AND ULULATE, OTHERS THROW TAMBOURINES,
BIBLES AND BABIES IN THE AIR.

DISCIPLE 1:
Fifteen Billion, is it Rand, Pula or USA?
He doesn't look Usa-friendly to me.

DISCIPLE 2:
What a fuss!
Fifteen Billion, even in Zimbabwean dollars, is still a lot of money.

Farmer whispers something to the preacher

PREACHER:
(*Stroking cheque with his fingers playfully*)
This good man of God has a word for you,
His Highness here says he has great plans to prosper us all,
Over to you, Sir.

FARMER:
(*Rubbing his palms together*) On June the twenty seventh
Something great and momentous will happen in our land
It will be the day for our historic break-through.
You will be asked to choose between me and some sly fox,

I implore you to stand by me Farmer-
The keeper of orphans and widows.
(The congregation applauds and jubilates).
EXIT FARMER

DISCIPLE 2:
Farmer has the prophet's voice,
While he was speaking
I saw his head rise to the clouds
And his shoulders block out the sun.

DISCIPLE 1:
I had a similar vision too.
Block the sun you say, that's a bad sign,
Did you see the head of brass and the feet of clay?
I don't like his temper, anyway.

DISCIPLE 2:
You are wearing your frock inside out;
and reading your visions back to front.
Temper temper, you cry
But therein lies his strength.
You don't expect the prince
To behave like pop-eye, do you?

DISCIPLE 1:
Remember we have two princes;
Don't believe Farmer until you have listened to Hunter,
Twins can say the same thing using the same words

But meaning three different things.

DISCIPLE 2:
Choosing between them I will go for Farmer's firm father-figure;
His home grown wisdom is a quality we should admire.

DISCIPLE 1:
Aha-a, there comes the gaity Hunter!
How gleams his arrows in the sun!
See, just see how broad and bold his chest is
Like the great wall of Kariba.
A-woo, how ripple the huge muscles
That can wrestle down a galloping buffalo!

Disciple 2:
Talk of the devil...

PREACHER:
Shhh shh, let's hear what he has to say.
And what's that protruding from his *nhava*?
(To the Hunter) O welcome! Welcome Sir!
With the help of divine grace, I foresaw your coming
Even *before* you appeared on the horizon!
Welcome! Welcome, we know you have a word for us,
Over to you, Sir.

HUNTER:
(Puts his bow down) Thank you. Thank you very much.

Excuse me bishops, deacons, comrades and Sunday
scholars;
All gathered here to pick heaven's manna.
I have come to make it possible
That with two loaves and five fish
Everyone will go to work every morning
Leaving refuse bins groaning with left-over's.

DISCIPLE 2:
(*In a low voice, to Disciple 1*)
Our minute of silence is over
Still I can't get a slice of his logic.
There must be something fishy in it.

DISCIPLE 1:
(*Whispering*) Give him a chance.
The ear is not filled with listening.

DISCIPLE 2:
(*Whispering*) Hear him! He thinks he is the Messiah,
What a blasphemy!

DISCIPLE1:
(*Whispering*) Even if you were born to criticize
At least you must listen first.

HUNTER:
These arms that tear the jaws of lions
Have no hesitation to tear Satan's jaw, too

And being amply scripture-literate,
For the church's twenty-seventh jubilee
I donate this horn of rhinocerous.
(*He hands the nhava to the preacher together with some papers*).
THE PEOPLE APPLAUD.

PREACHER:
Royalty is with us today!
What a rare gift we have got!
And this blessed servant of God has a bit of advice-
This is our very own prince
In whom we are pleased, listen to him!

HUNTER:
People, my people! I have a great love for you,
Farmer is my very own brother,
I shared my mother's womb with him for nine months
Therefore, I know him better than any of you.
When I say he's up to no good, it's not because I hate him
But that I don't want to see you fall into callous hands.
Give your support to Hunter and you will reap all the profits.

The people clap hands, Hunter picks up his bow and exits, a satisfied look on his face.

DISCIPLE 2:
Hunter who? That poacher you call a hunter!
Wasn't trafficking rhino-products banned?
And those papers, they don't look genuine to me.

DISCIPLE 1:
I don't see where Hunter goes wrong.
He has just doled on us a huge dollop of honey
And our church is none the poorer-
Unlike some political tourists who just come to our kingdom
With wide eyes like dragon flies
And the nectar-sipping mouths of butterflies.

DISCIPLE 2:
Your Hunter is the very political tourist you talk of,
Very suspect indeed.
More over God is not fascinated with flowers
Or captivated with combs of honey.
Him being the maker of the soil that feeds the flower
And the bee that brews the honey.

PREACHER:
Hallelujah! You all say the truth,
Only that you are standing back to back
And hiding each from the other's face;
But the richer and sweeter truth
Is that dollar and horn are now ours,
So let's wait for the said June in peace.
[END OF ACT ONE]

ACT TWO SCENE 1

In a classroom, a teacher of about fifty years of age, in graduation cap and gown, is standing before a class of students in the middle of a lesson on the subject called Politics and Poly-tricks which is about current affairs. It's nearly midday.

TEACHER:
O Yes, Clever give us your essay.

CLEVER:
(*Standing*) Thank you, sir.
Here is a tale of two short-men as told by a tall man who claims he tells no tall stories.
A man called Shorty of Resources has been found guilty of causing stand-stills in our productive industry. Mr Shorty of Resources is accused of creating a workforce with no work, a rich people without any wealth and any educated people lacking in knowledge. However, some say it's only a scape-goat; our good-old Shorty of Resources is just as *in-no-cent* as you and me.
It is another Shorty, Shorty of Shame who has been stealing progress and replacing it with reports in our cabinet ministers. Thus it remains to be seen whether the woes faced by the people are a result of Shorty of Resources or the other Shorty, Shorty of Shame.
I rest my case. Thank you. (*He sits, the class claps hands*).

TEACHER:

Yes, Buddy; good writing, but Mahatma Gandhi's quotes on work would have enhanced your essay. Alright everybody, our homework question for today is:
"If Rudeness and Politeness are two adjacent places, How is it that the distance from Rudeness to Politeness is long, whilst the return trip, from Politeness to Rudeness is several times shorter?"

FUTURE:
Which book, Sir?

TEACHER:
Chapters two and three in the book 'Nharoics, the Art of Argument", by Professor Shekanovitch Diraninsky.
Okay Debating Club, now is your time, Let's see if you can push-start a diesel train that has no engine!

FUTURE:
(*Standing*) Our debate topic is:
"By what unit do we measure an argument?"
Methinks in Kgs and tons like all things which have weight.

PROMISE:
I believe an argument is measured in Kilometres like all lengths.

CLEVER:
I think in hours and minutes, years or even decades Like all things that consume time.

TEACHER:
Alright, Clever, Future thinkers full of Promise
But Shekanovitch Diraninsky, 1971-edition says:
An argument is measured in 'Fools'
Since these are what determine its length.
There you are, my young friends;
Think twice before you add a *fool* to an argument.
Alright, Clever, give us the vote of thanks.

CLEVER:
(*Standing*) Thank you Sir for giving us
A coach-roach's eye-view of arguments,
But let me hasten to say good day to you all
Before I ignite an argument of forty fools,
Once more thank you.

The lunchtime bell rings. The pupils Exit the classroom. Enter a small boy who runs to the teacher and hands him an office-white paper. It's a circular letter. The teacher reads:

TEACHER:
(Reading) "Both Prince Hunter and Prince Farmer will be holding rallies in your area. Please be advised to prepare your pupils to recite poems and act dramas in their honour. You and your children are required to attend without fail. Please comply with this directive. Yours Commissar"
(shakes his head)
Little children at political rallies!
Another form of child abuse
Isn't that turning them into child soldiers armed with hatred?

Ha! Why don't politicians leave children alone? (He *throws down the letter but on second thoughts picks and pockets it, shaking his head*).

EXIT THE TEACHER

ACT TWO SCENE 2

Hunter and Farmer have just held rallies in different venues but there have been some noisy confrontations. On the street, a short man comes running; he is pursued by a tall man. The short man stops and draws a sword; the tall man pulls out his, too. They circle and glare at each other like two cockerels in a fight.

TALLMAN:
Supporters of Hunter do not deserve to live!
You are the scum of the Earth all of you.

SHORTMAN:
To be scum or not, I will always go for Hunter.
Denounce him from the top of a hill
Denounce him from the bottom of the sea
I will always go for Hunter, that's final.

TALLMAN:
Common sense eludes you,
Farmer is the true son of the soil,
It's folly to follow Hunter, a prodigal son
Whose face we barely know.

SHORTMAN:
Your common sense is as common as nonsense,
My allegiance lies in Hunter who has friends in many lands
And a good influence here and abroad.

TALLMAN:
Short-man, do not be short in the brain as well,
Why auction your birthright for a plate of porridge?
What good will those friends in foreign lands do?
You expect them, in your dwarfish mind,
To come here and make our wives pregnant for us, heh?
For that I shall stretch your imagination,
If not your neck, to a higher level.

SHORTMAN:
Tall-man, do not exaggerate your height
Then underestimate the distance to the ground.
Bamboo man with a brain but no mind,
Listen a little to the cackling of your straw-bones
When even a slight breeze touches your knees;
I can finish cutting across your shins with karate chops
Before your eyes pop out of the clouds to see what I'm doing.

TALLMAN:
This is gonna be a tall-order for you, snorty Shortie
Because I'm going to write of your short life
The world's shortest short-story!

SHORTMAN:
Your folly is taking its toll on you.
In short you could do better to show me
The difference between to fall and to collapse.

TALLMAN:
Why minimize myself by explaining anything in short?
I'm neither short sighted nor short of ideas.
No tall-man ever looked *up* at a short-man.

SHORTMAN:
A tall-man lying horizontally is not very tall to me.
I possess plenty of short-cut upper-cut ways
To bring a tall man's nose level with his toes.

TALLMAN:
You talk of toes because your eyes are near to them.

SHORTMAN:
Stay warned, you two-legged spider!

TALLMAN:
Ho ho ho-o! I a spider?
Listen, Fly, and listen carefully:
A green bomber entering a Blair toilet
May be forgiven for thinking it's a five-star hotel,
But a fly that dares test my nets
Will soon join its ancestors
Who scored well but lost the game.
Fly, little Fly, get yourself fast
To the grand safari lodge of the bush toilet!

THEY START FIGHTING FIERCELY.

[ENTER PREACHER CLASPING BIBLE TO HIS CHEST]

PREACHER:
[To himself] Surely these people will kill each other.
Only the Holy Spirit can break these chains of Satan,
But, which verse shall I read to cool their tempers?
Let me read 'a kingdom divided unto itself will not stand'.
No, let me read the beatitudes instead.
[In a loud voice] *Blessed are those who*...............

THERE IS A SUDDEN CRACK OF GUNFIRE. THE SHORTMAN SCREAMS AND FOLDS OVER IN MORTAL PAIN, HIS DYING MOANS ARE DROWNED BY THE TALL MAN'S RAUCUOUS VOICE HOWLING VICTORIOUSLY.

TALLMAN:
(Laughing) Ha, ha, ha, hola hey!
You bring a sword to fight me?
Feel the shot of the short-gun Short-man!
(He sprints away)

PREACHER:
------ *cry for they shall be consoled.*
(He goes to the fallen man)
It is written, the Good Samaritan helped a man on the road.

Enter Farmer and Hunter from different ends of the road. Farmer is limping; his shirt is torn and bloody. He is dusty all over and there are scraps of grass in his hair. Hunter's face is twisted in a frown and there are blood stains on his shirt too. Both do not see the preacher. They stand a distant from each other as if fearing one another.

FARMER:
(*Groaning*) Hunter, you are not my brother anymore.
I can see living with baboons in the thickets
Has taught you not a few tricks,
But your bandits have failed their attempt on my life,
Your dissidents have destroyed my winter wheat!

HUNTER:
Bah! Should I weep that Farmer has refused to be my brother?
Dissidents you say? Well, I don't breed dissidents and bandits.

FARMER:
You kid no one.
But hear me now
You shall set foot at The Tower of Dzimbahwe
Only to admire the chevrons but never to rule!

HUNTER:
That will have to be seen.
Farmer, the smell of unwashed gumboots
Wafts out of your mouth each time you mention my name.
I can see there are new compost heaps at your farm,
But I know they are graves of my people.
(*To himself*) Ha Politics!
I miss even a good night's sleep,

My life was better while I shot warthog,
(Aloud) But do not think I fear you!

FARMER:
Where did you see graves?
You are making it up to divert people from your sabotage.
Oh, my very promising winter crop, all of it wrecked!
The bread of the nation, all of it destroyed!
Zounds! I will kill someone this year!
(He *starts walking away but sees the preacher still crouching beside the body, and advances upon him.*
To Preacher pointing with finger)
Now I see you and your congregation
Found good use for fifteen billion dollars
And not any for my words.
Not even once did I see your face at my rallies
I'm considering that you pay me back.

PREACHER:
(Trembling) Y-yes, Your Highness I--- I---

(Farmer walks away ranting about his winter crop, Hunter strides to the Preacher)

HUNTER:
Aha-a good fellow, here we meet again.
How does rhino horn money taste?
I can see your fingers are well shaped for writing cheques

And not for bandaging my bloodied knees on the day I'm savaged
by barbarians;
But If I demand that you pay me back
Maybe you and your followers will appreciate
That I didn't pick the horn off a supermarket shelf.

PREACHER:
My good lord…

HUNTER:
I don't like people who call me good. *(He walks away)*

PREACHER:
(Weeping) U-huu, if this was a trap then it was a good one.
Where will my poor flock find fifteen billion? A rhino horn?
Oh my father in heaven have mercy!
Surely this will take us two years of Sundays to pay up this debt.
A year of Sundays for Farmer
A year of Sundays for Hunter
What a big debt for a poor congregation!
Repaying it will not differ from purchasing the Devil with weekly
instalments.
I pray the people will not decide to liquidate the church,
And Farmer, Lord save me from Farmer!
He looked so eager to invite the auctioneers.
(He exits leaving the body on the road side)

ACT TWO SCENE 3

In the palace the king sits pensively with his head in his hands. He is very sad; news of his sons' violent conduct and fatal incidents has reached him. The two young-men have not been seen in the palace for a long time but they are being spotted far from home hanging out with some strange faces. Now he has summoned them for a meeting.

KING:
(To himself, pacing around the room with hands on his back)
Yes, my *Sahwira* was right, my children have changed.
The politician's bug has bitten them,
Now they are power hungry and sick.
Hunter no more smiles those great smiles of his that could charm a python.
Farmer whistles not anymore those care-free carols he loved to hang on his lips while he worked his crops.
Now my once handsome boys have such weird faces
That look like scary artifacts of voodoo used by witches to induce terror.
Surely the vipers of the east and the vampires of the west
Have contrived to turn my sons into brutish monsters.

ENTER HUNTER AND FARMER AT ONCE BUT USING DIFFERENT DOORS

HUNTER:
O what ails thee, Grandson of Munhumutapa?

You walk alone talking of vampires and vipers.

FARMER:
Surely something is the matter
O Inyangani the everlasting rock
What mischievous problem provokes
That gleam of anger in your eye?

KING:
As if you do not know!
Tell me, Farmer; tell me, Hunter
From what jungle-book
Are you two reading your manners?

FARMER:
Ask Hunter who dances with apes
Down mountain sides every day.

HUNTER:
Much better than dancing with donkeys.

KING:
Now you shut up and listen to me!
Sit down! *(The twins sit)*
If you respect me as your father,
Then you should be wary to shame me with your actions.
Every day I hear of your tyranny to my people
Every day I hear of the mayhem on the streets.

FARMER:

It's not me, father, it's ...... [*The king motions him to shut up*]

KING:

You are too clever for your own good young man.
Now tell me, Farmer, who are those ungentle men
That visit you by night like bats?

FARMER:

Just customers for my crops coming ...

KING:

I'm aware of all your hare-brained tactics,
They are all right here in my hand.
And you Hunter,
Who are those nasty looking people around you,
And what is it you spend hours plotting behind doors?

HUNTER:

Just some business associates....

KING:

Boy, if I were a fool I'd not have been king all these years.
I know every little bit of your plots, young man.
Now here is a piece of advice for you both.
Be careful, very careful that your so-called allies
Are not foxes out to fool you.
Some of those bible-toting missionaries
Are just pirates disguising banditry with the frock.

Tolerate not the buccaneering businesses
Bent to turn this green oasis of our country
Into a stadium for their wars.
Violence I will not tolerate.

HUNTER:
It's Farmer's fault who ...

FARMER:
Who what? it's your jungle tacti...

KING:
Not a word from you two!
Oh, what sin did I commit
To sentence one poor country to two deaths?
But listen to this, unclever ones,
I will leave The Crown of the state
In the hands of a leader rather than a ruler.
I have the mind not to hand down the crown at all,
Now, off you go and behave yourselves!

Farmer and Hunter sullenly leave their seats and walk towards the door, they meet Mazwi-The Poet at the door. He looks as if he had been lurking nearby. They scowl at him suspiciously. Mazwi makes a rude action at them, comes in, sits beside the king and the two are soon lost in talk.

ACT TWO SCENE 4

On a deserted road enter Mazwi-the-poet; he carefully scans in all directions then starts walking strangely, staggering as if drunk.

MAZWI:
(*Singing*) A merry-gun in the Armoury-car
You love to war, but we don't.
I don't mind getting lost in Gonarezhou
But to be rediscovered in Guangzhou, no!
Brutish fellows in distant isles
Back to your sa-nato-rium with your irrussianal guys
I would like to see Hunter and Farmer kiss each other
Goodbye (*he hears footsteps and hides*).

ENTER HUNTER WITH A FOREIGN-LOOKING FRIEND AND SOME BODY-GUARDS

HUNTER:
Ha! The contest is harder than I imagined!
Farmer covers his weak parts like a pangolin;
He now sleeps with one eye open
In one hundred and one secret nests.
And to push him is like pushing a mountain;
What would I not pay to secure The Crown?

PAL:
It's very easy, so very easy.

We can make it happen for a little price in gold.
A revolution is a messy and tiresome business
And the gates of palace are built strong to withstand an irate mob,
But there is always a wee gap in the wall
To lizard your way into state-house.

HUNTER:
Gold is not a problem we have it lining even our pavements.
(*Stopping to listen*) I think I caught a rustle in the grass.
(*They stop and listen but everything is quiet, Hunter sees a foot print in the sand*)
Eh, he was here just now, Old Mazwi was here
His step falls with this rickety rhythm that leaves foot prints like question marks on the path.

MAZWI ABANDONS HIS COVER, JUMPS ONTO THE SCENE,

MAZWI:
I may have rickets in my knees,
But you have them in the mind!
Fret not nor snigger,
Foolish nigger
Befriending a gold digger.
Good morning, Sirs!

HUNTER:
(*Clapping hands*) Yippee! Good rhythm!

Another one of those nonsense poems of yours,
When will you go back to *Twinkle twinkle little star?*

MAZWI:
Very soon, very very soon,
To *Baa baa Black Sheep'* as well,
But there are two lizards I must sort out first;
You have the face of one of them.

HUNTER:
If you speak like that again
Then I shall not be your friend.

MAZWI:
So be it, I would rather hug myself
And sing a dirge the remaining days
Than be friends with you.

HUNTER:
You are nuts!
(He disappointedly walks away followed by his pal and body guards. The poet dismisses them with a back-hand gesture)

MAZWI:
All that politicians dream of
Is for poets to sing them praises and worship;
But I shall be the discordant voice to grate on their conscience
With th'abrasive tunelessness of Truth.

(He sees Farmer and hides)

FARMER IS COMING ALONG WITH THREE OTHER PEOPLE; ONE A STRANGER THE OTHER TWO BODYGUARDS. THEY ARE HEADING IN THE DIRECTION HUNTER HAS TAKEN.

FARMER:
I am the farmer;
I put hoe to the ground, my own scepter of miracles,
And up-rises green plants like holy spirits.
Can't I do the same and cultivate a crop of supporters
That over-fills my silos with votes?

CONSULTANT:
That is the children's cartoon version of politics;
The pragmatic thing to do is to undress the opponent
As a way to address the populace.

FARMER:
But Hunter has turned himself into a fleeting shadow,
So impossible to pin down.
His new passion is setting booby traps in my path.
The world I'd surely pay to snare that elusive mongoose.

CONSULTANT:
No need to pay the world, Chum,
Just a share of Mutare diamonds to grease some palms.

FARMER:
Anything my friend

CONSULTANT:
My friend, listen to me carefully.
Gentlemen may be snared with sex,
Ladies baited with purses,
Every being is prepared to sell themselves out at a certain price.
Hunter is not an omnipotent god,
A few gorilla tactics will tumble him down.

MAZWI:
(*Leaping from hiding*)
Hoe hyes you Highness!
Mister Dirty Tactics,
Our diamonds are no currency to buy Diablos!
Go fill your silos with clean votes
We want peace, not gorilla tactics here!

FARMER:
(*Recovering from being startled*)
Out of my ears, you tongue-loose idiot!
Your words are as foul as public snoring,
Spares my ears from that voice of a tractor!
(*He walks away with his friends*).

Mazwi:
(*Laughing*) Ha ha haa he-hee!

Sayer of the ruthless truth, licensed to scold!
Even donkey-skinned dictators wince
From the crackling whip of walloping words.
From today on I shall become the unbecoming opposition within the opponents,
And the ruler that rules the unruly elements into straight lines,
And let's see who will have the last laugh!
[HE EXITS]

ACT THREE: SCENE 1

On the road. It is mid-morning. Hunter is walking along in the company of his friend and body-guard. They hear a melodious singing in the air.

HUNTER:
Oh foolish me, I had forgotten that it's parents' day at school
today; let's go see Blue-Necktie's latest pranks;
Who knows, I might catch an elephant of support there.

They turn into the school yard. As they enter the school, Hunter spots Farmer sitting among the VIPs he goes and sits there too but a distance from his brother. The teacher in his graduation gown and cap, is conducting the choir. He is beating and waving at the air with wide ecstatic gestures.

CHOIR:
Dai hudi-i-ki hwaidzokerwawo
Ndaingewo-o nha-a-si ndadzo-o-ka
Paunha-a-na, pauto-mbi
Ndaiti kana ndoseka
Ndoti nemavende nyechu!

THE PEOPLE CHEER AND APPLAUD HAPPILY.

HUNTER:
[*To himself*] Hey, how Blue-Necktie basks
In the adoration of those little infants!
Is there a better way to win the world
Than to be loved by children?

FARMER:

(To himself) See Blue-Necktie, though in fading suit,
How those toddlers shower him with a genuine love unpolluted
with adult lies!
Can there be a vainer victory
Than to win the entire universe
And yet be unloved by children?

MISTRESS OF CEREMONIES:

[*Using microphone*]
Oh yes, let's give a pam pam to the choir.
Now here is a grade six drama, enjoy it!
A group of boys and girls start arranging themselves into the shape of Africa.
They are holding hands while singing.

CHILDREN:

(singing) Africa unite, Africa unite!
Unite for the benefit of your children
We're moving right out of Babylon
And we are going to our motherland
How good and how pleasant it'd be
To see the unification of all Africans!

Two smart men appear from the left one has the word '*ally*' the other '*advisor*' printed on the chests of their t-shirts. They stop a distance from the Children of Africa.

ALLY:

What are the African children doing today?

ADVISOR:

Singing odes and anthems to their continent.

ALLY:

Oh, that's boring, very boring
persuade them to play *chisveru*
Or the *blame* game, its better you know.

Ally whispers something in the ear of one child while advisor does the same to another child. Immediately the children start pointing fingers at each other and chasing one another around making quarrelling noises. Ally and advisor depart then come back after a short while.

ALLY:

What are the African Children doing today?

ADVISOR:

They have started playing pinch-pinch

ALLY:

A-ah, monotonous game, give them catapults.

Advisor and ally walk away. The children start shooting each other with slings. They wail and cry as they shoot and dodge flying rocks. After a while advisor and ally come back. Each is carrying a curious baggage.

ADVISOR:

Any news from the Dark Continent?

ALLY:

They are shooting each other with pistols, wonder where they got them.

ADVISOR:

Aagh, *pistols*! Not so effective, why not donate them a ship load of those 1947 AK's we no longer need?

Advisor and ally relinquish their baggage to the children. The children distribute rifles to each other. Sounds of gunfire erupt. The children start running and hiding aiming guns at each other. Sobbing and crying increases. Some children fall down dead, some are crawling all over the place in pain. Ally and advisor exit on the right then resurface from another angle.

ADVISOR:

Hallo, what are the Africans up to today?

ALLY:

Mangling each other with tanks.

ADVISOR:

Bah! Primitive warfare, those tanks were in fashion way back in '45,
Sell them some of those missiles in our armoury.
They can pay us in cash or in kind -
In diamonds or simply in oil.

Ally and advisor walk away. The noise grows louder, there is smoke rising from the stage. The firing of weapons continues, one by one the children fall and die. Finally, there is no movement and the noise dies down only the smoke continues billowing. Ally and advisor re-appear wearing smart business suits. They stand at the edge of the mess.

ALLY:

(laughing) Where are the Africans with their odes and anthems now?

ADVISOR:

They have turned their countries into wastelands; barbaric lot,

All they are good at are ethnic wars and bloody genocides.

ALLY:

Yah, the obvious third world story; doesn't concern us.

Tell you what; we have just realized 200% profit in six months!

Hoola! Our shareholders will be ululating in the boardroom!

Come to the beach, Buddy

And let's enjoy a few drinks, cheers!

ADVISOR:

Yeah, why not? (*Ally and Advisor leave the stage arm in arm sipping drinks*)

The grade six drama ends. The audience claps hands. Amid the fanfare Hunter and Farmer look at each other and frown.
EXEUNT ALL

ACT THREE SCENE 2

On the road, Hunter and Farmer are coming from opposite directions. Each is in the company of followers. In the distance both of them spot the teacher wearing his graduation gown, he is walking on a side–road coming into the main road, a plastic container sloshing with some beer hangs in his hand. He is stopping every few steps to take a drink from the container. From the way he fumbles he is apparently drunk. It is nearly evening.

HUNTER:
(*To his pal*) Very good, there comes Blue-Tie,
If only I could capture his support,
Then the scholars would follow his Socrates-face
Right into the back of my nets.
Let's hope he's not brain-dead with *seven-days*.

PAL:
Yes, it's a good move to court Mr Books,
His Pythagoras theorems will show us the way
To romp home to a square victory.

FARMER:
(*Coming from the opposite direction, to his consultant*)
Who have we got here? O yes the teacher!
If only I could harness the teacher's tongue
Then all the love his children have for him
Would come to me too.

CONSULTANT:
Yes, good observation.

FARMER:
You know what, I sometimes think:
To be loved by the old folks
Is to be smiled upon by life;
To be loved by young men and women
Is to be loved by the world;
But to be adored by children
Is to be loved by God himself.
With all the youths on our side
Our party would be strongest,
And my life would attain a class of its own.

CONSULTANT:
(Laughs) Slowly becoming like the poet, hey!
Ever so philosophical *(laughs again)*
But, anyway, good strategy,
Go ahead and transplant the chalkman into your garden
His Archimedes Principles will show us the skill
To displace the opponent in the high-density areas.

FARMER:
But now, how to dredge him out of homemade malt!

THEY MEET.

HUNTER:
Aha- a welcome, welcome, Rabbi!
Surely today is a blessed one for great minds to meet.

FARMER:
Hallo, Mwalimu,
I have always longed for a word with you.

TEACHER:
(His voice a bit slurred)
O thank you, your Majesties.
(He pauses a while tries to salute but he is unsteady on his feet, he tries to brush past)

FARMER:
Easy Mr Chalk-Man, just a minute of your time.

TEACHER:
Pardon me if I appear to be in a hurry
Trying to reach some unmarked books in time.

FARMER:
You are hurrying in your mind
But your knees are surely in a slow motion.
That aside, be patient; it`s all in your own interest.
I have hatched a dollar-wise scheme
That will see your noble profession reclaim its glitter.

TEACHER:

Sorry to disappoint you, Your Honour,
But if its poverty then I have known it long enough
That it no longer hurts.

HUNTER:
Every nation that snubs its teachers
Posts decades of darkness into the future.
Come, Socrates, come with me;
Light the path to our common destiny.

TEACHER:
I don't know with you, Sir,
My own destination is evening class,
Of course we'd love to include you in our night-school.

HUNTER:
You seem to have forgotten who we are.

TEACHER:
(*He lifts the container to his lips, takes a long draw*)
Not so, Your Highness, I know you well,
My regards to Chibwe The everlasting Rock.
Please allow me to proceed in peace.

FARMER:
Proceed in peace, indeed!
The problem with you teachers
Is that you reason too much.
But let me school you a bit,

Inside you books you need to be right
But out in this world you need to be correct.
We know you have been polluting children with politics
Never attended our rallies, too.
We don't want to make things nasty for you, do we?

TEACHER:
(*Is silent for a moment*)
It's unfortunate that I seem to be misunderstood
But I always teach that which I must.
And I must protect myself and little babes
From being lured into classrooms of another kind.

FARMER:
What! Is this sleep-talking or what!
Do you know no one ever talks to us like *that*?
You are stinking of beer!

HUNTER:
If you talk in that drunken way again,
We may charge you with misconduct, or is it improper association?
Moreover, you have been drunk on duty.

TEACHER:
(*burps*) Please allow me to proceed in peace.

HUNTER:
Okay friend, we will talk it over,

But do sup with me tonight on liver of warthog
And South Pole honey
Which my imported bees brewed on winter flowers.
(*He draws closer to the teacher*)

FARMER:
Alright, Socrates, business aside,
Come with me to my gardens of grapes,
And plantations of bananas and sugar cane.
From my cellars a keg of wine to top it all

The joy of the experience is enough to kill a man,
Come Socrates,
you won't regret it. (*He inches nearer to the teacher*)

TEACHER:
Sorry Sirs, I might sound like sour grapes, but my class of night scholars must be getting impatient.

HUNTER:
Your greatest weakness is that you tend to calculate too much!

Hunter grabs at the teacher's graduation gown and tries to pull him to his side. Farmer clasps on it too, pulls in the opposite side and a tug-of-war starts. After a while the baffled teacher wriggles out of the gown and stands aside watching as the twins continue to wrestle over it. The offending cloth rips into two.

TEACHER:
(*Recovering*) Ai! I didn`t expect this!

On second thoughts, I'd rather follow my shadow.

GREATLY ANGERED, HUNTER AND FARMER THROW THE GOWN-PIECES AT THE TEACHER'S FEET AND STRIDE AWAY IN OPPOSITE DIRECTIONS WITH THEIR FOLLOWERS SULLENLY BEHIND THEM.

(Takes a drink from the plastic container. To himself)
Now that I have angered those terrible twins
My life will no longer be the same again.
What is it I must do to buy back my freedom?
Ii-i *Farmer!* Farmer doesn't take no for an answer.
Should I go bananas with Farmer?
And risk my mind getting gnawed by cane-mice?
South Pole honey- brewed on winter flowers-
That must be very sweet;
Should I carry my chalk soaked self to Hunter-
Who would rather choke on gun-powder smoke
Than sneeze on chalk-dust?
Maybe I should just go home
And mark my pupils' books.

The sun sets with the figure of the teacher hunched by the road-side, brooding deeply.

ACT THREE: SCENE 3

Early morning on the road. It's one of those rare moments when Farmer and Hunter are thrown together by circumstances. They are in the company of a soldier and are going to different places.

FARMER:
(Pointing at the figure of a man in sleeping position)
Who is it that lies there
In a still peace that is akin to heavenly bliss?

HUNTER:
A silent and still peace
Which even we the princes
Do only dream of but never afford.

THEY WALK CLOSER TO INVESTIGATE

FARMER:
Ah, it's the teacher! [*Laughing*]
Ha-ha-haa! Whose *seven-days'* brew is it,
That knocks out my good teacher so?

HUNTER:
Ha! He seems to me to be
In a silent and still peace which no-one adores.

SOLDIER:
Stone cold, ee- ah; he`s dead! What happened?
Who killed him?

HUNTER:
A! dead?

FARMER:
It looks like suicide.

HUNTER:
Uugh, God forbid, Blue-tie no more?

FARMER:
It could be hunger that killed him.

HUNTER:
Doesn't look so to me.
All these wounds!
And what's this stuffed in his mouth?

SOLDIER:
Chalk-pieces! Ate chalk out of poverty?

HUNTER:
What's this? Ah, look at this,
A biro sticking in his heart wound!

FARMER:
Maybe his errors corrected themselves that way;
Live by the pen die by the pen.

SOLDIER:
Maybe he___.

HUNTER:
You shut up! And hold your gun the right way!
(*To Farmer*) What shall we do now?

FARMER:
Nothing.

HUNTER:
He wasn't actually a bad fellow.

FARMER:
And you mind what your big mouth says;
We never saw this body, right?

HUNTER:
(*Ruefully*) He wasn't actually a bad fellow.

SOLDIER:
Strange bed fellows!

HUNTER:
I told you to S.H.U.T- U.P!
Soldier shrinks back.

THEY WALK AWAY.

Enter Mazwi, who has been following and observing the group under-cover. Sees the body. He goes and kneels beside it. He closes the copses' eyes and mouth and folds its arms.

MAZWI:

[Lamenting to himself]

O what has politics done to a gentleman?
As if poverty was not punishment enough.
Now when any nation is ruled
By those who ran away from corrections,
Common sense dies a loud and shameful death.
Sorry to you, my long suffering friend,
Our country has surely gone to wooden-beings.
(*He walks away*).

ACT 3: SCENE 4

In the palace, the king is having some food. The radio is on and it's the lunch time news. The king looks a bit absent minded and is not paying much attention to the news.

RADIO:
Sad news we have just received says unknown-assailants visited the teacher last night and extorted from our book man more than what he owed and owned. The teacher also known as Bluetie made headlines last year of living in dire poverty.

KING:
(absent mindedly, to himself)
Where does that leave my eternally-broke friend?
If only he could subsist less on malt beer...

RADIO:
His body was discovered this morning by children near the school rubbish pit...

KING:
His *body*? Ha, his body? He can't be dead!
(He stops eating, washes hands)
"Unknown-assailants" did the news say?
Hunter! Farmer! Be here right now!
Eish! This is the worst year to ache on my bones.

(The Twins hurry into Palace with eager looks, a soldier who waits outside the King's chamber enters behind them).

HUNTER AND FARMER:
(*Together expectantly*) Yes, I am here.
(*They take two seats facing the king*)

KING:
Please tell me, what does *unknown-assailants* mean?

THE TWO LOOK SHEEPISHLY AT EACH OTHER CONFUSED AT FIRST BUT THEY SOON REALISE WHAT THE KING IS IMPLYING.

HUNTER:
Ask Farmer who owns the dictionary
Of politics and mumbo-jumbo.

FARMER:
It`s your son Hunter, who brings home those lean words
Which have little flesh and a lot of bones.

KING:
Lord help me! The sentences of both of you!
By your crooked beaks and vulture looks
I can tell you have supped with witches.
Who are those *unknown-assailants* who are going about killing people?
I hear the teacher has been assassinated on the street.
Hee- hee! This time you have gone too far!
But let me remind you,

This kingdom and its shining crown were not conceived on the day
you were born and will not cease to exist without you.
I am not asking respect from you, I am demanding obedience.
I speak to you now *not* as your father
But as the sovereign king of this land.
I shall not have anyone turn The Tower of Nehoreka
Into a den of blood-thirsty demons,
No, I shall not have it!
And none of you shall climb the throne
By the ladder of human bones.
Till the twenty-seventh let me not hear of any bloodshed,
Or else I will be forced to make you regret.
Off you go and behave yourselves.
(*The Twins exit sullenly*).

THE KING IS LEFT BEHIND COGITATING.

ACT THREE: SCENE 5

Narrator: There is throwing of stones, bottles, spears and home-made bombs in the streets as mobs continue fighting, burning and looting. The King himself is ill with all the stress. Business is affected and some people stop going to work. Money is a problem and there is a scarcity of food. Only the new industry of violence thrives- churning out broken limps and mangled bodies.

ON THE ROAD IT IS A QUIET EVENING LIT BY MOONLIGHT. ENTER OLDWOMAN AND OLDMAN COMING FROM A BEERDRINK

OLDWOMAN:
[Singing] *Shuga yodhura, doro rodhura*
Zvinondodini kutova mavende
Ko kutonhodza gurokuro?
Nhasi ndatenga shana yembeva
Asi ambhuya vacho vanokakama
Vati pa-bhi-bhi-bhirioni
Ha-ha-ha hapana chenji.

OLDMAN:
(Singing, a distance behind the old woman)
Nyarara zvako Tiriri musikana asingachembere
Ndichakutengera mapatapata e-tu tririoni...

ANGRY VOICE:
Who are those who sing as if from the grave?

OLDMAN:
(*Stopping*) It`s us your old folks,
Trying our teething tongues and uttering gums
On these adages of fifteen digit numbers.

OLDWOMAN:
(*Stopping and tying her shawls; shouting
towards the source of the voice*)
My friend, how many zeros are in trillion?
Is it because they are mind-numbing
Why they called them numbers?
(*They start chuckling at their own jokes.*)

ANGRY VOICE
Varoyi!

*Something is thrown from the direction of the voice and lands between
Oldwoman and Oldman. It's a human head, freshly severed and still bleeding.*

OLDWOMAN
A dead head! Wau, jump on it!
Forget your age and borrow your boyhood sprint;
A dead head with a bloody grin, O I don`t like this!

OLDMAN:
You forget you are still so *be-youthful*
To make even dreadful hades smile!
Ignore the head and ride the wind home!

(They stumble hastily away, frightened)

ENTER MAZWI-THE-POET, HE SEES THE WEAPONS AND DEBRIS OF VIOLENCE LITTERING THE STREET, HE SEES THE BLOODY HUMAN-HEAD.

MAZWI:
[*Lamenting*] Gimme back my Zimbabwe of old or I die!
I shall never trust any politician again
Because politics killed my country.
Every politician's hobby is lying,
Every politician's walking stick is a gun
But they fight better whose weapon is peace.
Every bullet shot mourns the death of shame,
Every bomb swallowing a city with tall flames
Illuminates the grave pit-falls of power hunger.
(There is crack of gunfire, a bullet hits him on the shoulder, he falls then clambers back to his feet)
See; see, I stand here bleeding now,
But what has this bullet that hit me solved?
(He exits clutching shoulder)

ACT FOUR: SCENE 1

Farmer and hunter have been gradually amassing supporters. As the day of reckoning draws closer they are both beginning to get desperate and nervous. ENTER FARMER WITH FOLLOWERS-CUM-SOLDIERS. SOME OF THEM HAVE GUNS. THERE IS A FOREIGN LOOKING INDIVIDUAL AMONG THEM.

FARMER:
[*Chanting*] Zimbabwe the great!

FOLLOWERS:
(*Together*) Shining palace on a hill!

FARMER:
(*Chanting*) Mukoko wegonera uzere neuchi!

FOLLOWERS:
(*Together*) Kachuru kazere neshwa dzako!

FARMER:
(*Stopping*) Has anyone seen the rabid jackal lately?

FOLLOWERS:
We haven`t seen him for days.

FARMER:
Then that long tailed beast must be somewhere
Stealing and stashing nuts for winter

Or digging tunnels under my feet like a crazy mole.

CONSULTANT:
Imagine if Hunter were to win
How noisy his laughter would be!
All the rich mines will be under his feet.
To get the best out of an unfair man
Use fairly unfair means.

FARMER:
Yes you are right;
Hunter cannot beat me in a straight match
And that he knows too well.

CONSULTANT:
Straight match, my foot!
If you're expecting straight matches,
Then you are in the wrong game, my friend,
Politics is brawn, *Politics* is bones and blood.

FARMER:
(takes a long moment of thinking, then a new idea brightens his face)
Yes, yes; why not cut a long story short?
And why didn't I think of this all along?
(Suddenly shouting orders to his soldiers)
Barrels to the left
Butts to the right
Toss the rule-book over your shoulder
And church-manners into the loo!

SOLDIER 1:
Are we retreating or advancing?

FARMER:
Throw the rule book over your shoulder
And son-in-law manners to the loo!
Now the son is the father of the king!
To the Tower, as the crow flies!

THE TROOPS GET INTO FORMATION. THEY EXIT TOWARDS THE LEFT MARCHING BRISKLY.

ENTER HUNTER FROM THE RIGHT WITH HIS OWN TRAIN OF FOLLOWERS. AMONG THEM IS AN IMPORTANT LOOKING MAN WITH A CLIPBOARD.

HUNTER:
(Addressing followers)
We are entering the moment called *never before,*
The time when we must do the undone
In order to undo the done.
Ha ha ha! *(Laughs cruelly)*
I hear the stomachs of big men rumbling with fright.
Farmer is the big man whose stomach is rumbling now.
Has anyone seen the barn owl lately?

FOLLOWERS:
(In unison) No-one has!

HUNTER:
That`s a bad cue then,
He must have gone to replenish his calabash of witchcraft
Too frightened to meet me head-on on a level ground.

PAL:
Bah! Level ground! levelled by who?
If your freedom fighters had waited for level ground
The Promised Land they'd never have reached.

HUNTER:
Meaning…?

PAL:
Imagine if Farmer were to beat you
How loudly he would celebrate!
He will be lord of the diamond mines
While you pick at the leavings of his table.
The options for you are either to sit and wait for chance
Or to go out and grab chance by the horns.

HUNTER:
Yes, Farmer is a coward
And cowards have dangerous minds,
He might be burying land mines at palace gates right now.

PAL:
Or doing something worse.

HUNTER
(*Thinks for a while, talking to himself*)
"Go out of my way,
Grab chance by the horns", Oh yes;
And why not fry a pig in its own fat?
Ahaa, welcome good idea!
(*Shouting suddenly in a terrifying voice, the people stop*)
Forgive me all ye weak ninnies,
Now I must put on my fighting cloak
To enter once more my heart of stone
And face the flying claws of a lion charging;
(*Commanding*) Barrels to the right
Butts to the left
Shoot bull- accurate at twitching heart!
To The Tower about turn!

SOLDIER 2:
Are we advancing or retreating?

HUNTER:
Yours is not to cry and ask why,
Yours is but to wrestle fire with fire
Beside your new king, Hunter the unburnable!
Blood and sweat there shall be but tears never!
(*The soldiers march into formation*).
Make way all ye men big and small
Here comes the *chu-chu train!*
EXIT HUNTER AND HIS TRAIN

ACT FOUR: SCENE 2

At the palace gates, from the gazebo, Mazwi scans the surrounding landscape. His hand is in bandages; he peers intently in the distance seeing a moving plume of dust. Looking in the opposite direction he sees another moving speck far on the horizon.

MAZWI:
(*To himself*) Is that a whirl wind in the east?
Isn't that a whirlwind in the west?
When last did we see two whirlwinds meet?
For all his wrinkles the poet has never seen it happen;
But those ill-winds are heading for The Tower.
Isn't that the face of Farmer floating in the dust
White as china-clay?
The way his eyes blink!
Like a three-eyed being looking for coin to steal.
(*He disappears into the Palace for a while then comes back to meet the mob*)
(*With raised voice*) Is nothing really something?
Hey, soldier, can you shoot down *nothing*?

SOLDIER:
Stand aside, you bagful of words!
The valiant Farmer will soon need a yapper
To sing rubbish and nonsense,
But for now, go hide your wrinkled face somewhere!
(*He shoves him aside; the poet goes into hiding, off stage*)

MILITIA MEN POUR INTO PALACE AND START SEARCHING FOR THE KING AND THE CROWN IN THE BACK GROUND. IN THE FORE GROUND FARMER IS PACING AROUND TALKING TO HIMSELF.

FARMER:
In six months I should start the agrarian reforms,
In which street shall I erect my statue?
But why is the palace so quiet?
A cabinet of ten ministers will be ideal.
It's high time I get a title for myself
Ah, but I can't be Tsar like a Russian;
Or Igwe like a Nigerian.
Field Marshal. Yes Field Marshal can do,
Honourable Field-Marshal Farmer; yah it carries weight.
But why is this taking so long?

THEY SEARCH THE ENTIRE PALACE THROUGHLY BUT FAIL TO FIND THE KING OR THE CROWN. THEY START MILLING OUTSIDE, THEIR HEADS HANGING SULLENLY.

SOLDIER:
(*saluting*) There is nothing, Sir, not even a trace.

FARMER:
What could have happened?
(*Starts weeping*) It must be Hunter,
The thief must be Hunter only!

Hunter, *aaah*! You biggest of all baboons;
You think you have beaten me to it,
That is the gravest mistake you've made;
Just tuck in your tail and give me *back* my crown,
Or else you shall rule only in the hills and caverns.
(*Commanding*) After the mandrill baboon, ho brave soldiers!
I want the crown in my hands before mid-day!

SOLDIER:
But, my Lord; it's already *after* midday.

FARMER:
Tsk! You stand there blinking eyes like digital clocks
While a baboon climbs cliff and kopje with my crown!
Shake your shins like bamboo sticks in the monsoon!

SOLDIER:
But Sir, which direction shall we take?

FARMER:
Run *north-south*!

SOLDIERS SCATTER IN ALL DIRECTIONS. EXIT FARMER.
THE POET COMES OUT OF HIDING AND CLIMBS UP THE
GAZEBO AGAIN. HE SCANS THE SURROUNDING
PLAINS AGAIN AND SEES ANOTHER MOB
APPROACHING.

MAZWI:

So one wild-wind goes and another one comes.
Isn't that Hunter who pushes himself hither
With his gait of hyena?
If he could ask the poet,
He'd save himself some pain;
But men like Hunter who spend all their time among animals,
Cannot understand the value of asking.

HUNTER:
Oh the poet again! It is bad luck
To see this black bard perched on palace gates.
Say not a word, tongue-twister.

MAZWI:
As if you recognize words enough to understand them.
Empty headed soon empty handed.

SOLDIER 2:
Enough of that hee-haw, we didn't come this far
To hear an owl hum to the moon…

MAZWI:
Aah, an owl indeed.

SOLDIER 2:
But you are short-listed,
King Hunter will soon need a tongue-loose rambler
To sing sagas and recite sonnets;
But for now go drop yourself down the loo!

(*He elbows him aside*).

SOLDIERS SATURATE THE ROYAL HOUSE AND START SEARCHING FOR THE KING AND THE CROWN IN THE BACK GROUND. IN THE FORE-GROUND HUNTER AWAITS THE CROWN.

HUNTER:
(*Sitting in the king's chair*)
You hold the crown gently, soldier
I don't want any finger-prints on it,
But why is the place in such a mess?
(*To himself, holding and admiring a kingly gown he found in one of the rooms]*
Umm, should I dress to match the gold patterns
Or the diamond studs in the hemline?
Is this the best robe that sits on me like my skin?
Save for my soldiers this place looks long deserted.
My first hundred-day plan
Will be to move the front gate, rename it Hunter's Portico,
Make it look east, to welcome the rays of dawn into my kingdom every morning.
But why are my lieutenants taking long to bring The Crown?

HUNTER'S SOLDIERS TURN THE PALACE UPSIDE-DOWN; THEY RANSACK IT IN EVERY IMAGINABLE PLACE. BUT, AS THEY RESIGN AND POUR OUT, THE AIR IS HEAVY WITH DISAPPOINTMENT.

MAZWI:

(*Reciting with exaggerated gestures, and rolling his eyes*)
Nhava izere mhepo, izere mhepo nhava!
I would like to take a closer look at *nothing*,
To examine *a lump of nothing* between thumb and forefinger
Like a hundred carat diamond shining with nothingness.
To push my head into this scintillating bubble full of *nothing*,
And to roll my big eyes inside that *nothing* place,
Packing all my findings into these bags of *nothing*
And, under the weight of nothing
Stagger home to a sad wife…

HUNTER:
Soldier, whip that fellow. (*A soldier complies*)

MAZWI:
Ah, Hunter, you too have changed?
Waa! You hurt my arm. (*He dashes away out of sight*)

HUNTER:
(*in weeping voice*) Aaa-gh Farmer, you father of vermin
Who washes his face in a dip-tank!
Listen to me the last time -
Yours is the jaw I surely would love to tear.
If you think you can steal the crown and get away with it,
Then you are mistaken!
Now you are plastering *my* crown
With fingers wet with cow dung!
Hear me now, hear me now!
When I start coming after you

You will realize that one furrow of sorghum
Would have paid you better than investing in slogans!
And what have you done with my King?
(Commanding) Soldier, get *my* crown now!

SOLDIER 2:
Which way shall we go?

HUNTER:
Go all the ways!
And don't just gape there while my crown is getting rusty in the manger of the donkey that knows nothing but braying at midnight!

SOLDIER 2:
Which way, Sir?

HUNTER:
Run *east-west*!

SOLDIERS SCATTER IN ALL DIRECTIONS, EXIT HUNTER AND THE FOREIGN LOOKING INDIVIDUALS. THE POET COMES OUT OF HIDING, DUSTS HIMSELF AND TAKES HIS PLACE IN THE GAZEBO.

MAZWI:
(To himself) where then is your cleverness?
Now you go ahead and rule, and let's see how you do it!
If you listen carefully when the old–folks speak
You will realize that the world needs no prophet.

It is good to solve problems
But it's best not to create them *(He exits)*.

ACT 4: SCENE 3

On the road, it is nearly evening. It's a few days after the incidents at the Tower of Mysteries. Oldman and Old Woman meet on the road.

OLDWOMAN:
Gecko, you haven't brought your wrinkles out to sun for a long time, in which cave are you cooped these days?

OLDMAN:
I'd rather have death come to me in my abode
Than go out and meet him in the street.
Strange things have happened to our land these past days.

OLDWOMAN:
Aye, but stranger things are afoot.
Did you hear the news, those kids Future and Promise are now husband and wife with a sagging pregnancy between them?

OLDMAN:
Little boys and girls rushing into marriage like that!

OLDWOMAN:
And also your nephew Clever is in the hands of the police with many crimes; doing drugs, house breaking and what not.

OLDMAN:
It was bound to come to that,

They haven't been schooling since their mentor got killed.
What should we expect if kids don't go to school?

(While they are still talking the girl Promise in school uniform, passes in front of them pushing an extra large belly, Old-man and Old-woman stare at her in silent wonder, shaking their heads)

OLDWOMAN:
Strange things are afoot indeed,
And did you hear the news that Old Chibwe cannot be found?

OLDMAN:
Old Chibwe? What are you talking about?

OLDWOMAN:
Yes, Old Chibwe has vanished from palace and not a living soul
knows where he is.

OLDMAN:
Ha! A king vanishing?

OLDWOMAN:
They say those two boys set their armies on The Tower,
And afterwards the King could not be found,
Maybe they abducted him or what.

OLDMAN:
A whole king vanishing!

OLDWOMAN:
Others say they failed to find the king so Chibwe must be alive somewhere.

OLDMAN:
The King of a land vanishing!

OLDWOMAN:
Those is the know say the twins are now arguing with their own shadows, going awry-minded.

OLDMAN:
O Nehanda`we, strike my eyes with blindness now
That I may not see the ends of this madness!
An entire king disappearing, just like that?

OLDWOMAN:
Yes, that's what your children have done.

OLDMAN:
(Shaking his head) *Ai-i baba`ngu Musikavanhu woye!*
Ndimi here makatipa mazivana aya asina matyira
Anovangarara kushamba mabori nemvura yeChirorodziva?

THEY WALK FOR A WHILE IN GRIEVED SILENCE THEN A PLAINTIVE VOICE WAFTS TO THEM. AT FIRST THEY IGNORE IT, BUT IT PERSISTS.

OLDMAN:

Whose voice is this I keep hearing?
Or are they only the owls of the bush
Who mock my poor ears with their howling?

OLDWOMAN:
No, there is a voice; I hear it, too
And the voice which I hear
is graven with chalk-sediments in its throat.

OLDMAN:
You might be right,
I too, discern school-bells in that voice,
Yet it can`t be Blue-Necktie
He being many weeks dead.

OLDWOMAN:
(*Stopping*) Shhh shhh, let`s listen.

VOICE:
I am the teacher whom you think you killed;
But as you can see, or as you can`t see,
You can`t kill me until I have taught you how.

OLDMAN:
Aaa, aah, let`s get back home, I don`t like this!
I buried that gentleman myself with these hands.

OLDWOMAN:
That is the voice of a spirit.

Wau, give me a pinch of your snuff.
(They start walking hastily away)

OLDMAN:
It's the teacher's voice, sure enough.
O how I wish he would come back
In voice and in person to teach us;
Our good nation would become a people again.

OLDWOMAN:
It's a pity, those in need schooling
Are the ones who hate it the most.
That fool among fools who does not see that he is naked
Is the worst one.

VOICE:
Thanks woman, for those words, thank you;
At least all is not lost with my people.
But woe unto them who broke my heart!
The dust of chalk shall sting their eyes,
And they shall wander lost forever
In a city that has no street names.

THE OLDMAN AND OLDWOMAN HURRY AWAY IN SILENCE FOR A WHILE:

OLDMAN:
Poor Blue-Tie, he's too offended to lie still in his grave.

OLDWOMAN:
It's a bad omen that kings vanish in broad daylight
And dead-men leave their rest-places
To harangue the living with grievous voices.
What shall we do then?

OLDMAN:
Tiriri i*we*, do not despair,
This thing we see our fathers called it:
The shining of darkness, the brilliance of ignorance,
It's that as a people we have been so unlucky
As to see two sunsets in one day
But all this will vanish like a bad dream
When the real dawn comes.
exit Old-man and Old-woman

ACT FOUR: SCENE 4

THE OLDMAN AND THE OLDWOMAN ARE SITTING CROSS LEGGED BEFORE THE SPIRIT-MEDIUM WHO IS CLAD IN ALL BLACK WITH A FEATHER CROWN ON HIS HEAD AND A STAFF IN HIS HAND.

ORACLE:
(*Talking snuff*) Give us your word, hoary-ones.
What is it that sets two chameleons on a long journey?

OLDMAN:
(Clapping hands)
Strange and horrifying things have happened
At Dzimbahwe,
We come to you, O Great Sangoma
That you may sweep the thorns from our path.
Your infants are now afraid to go out and play
And at night their sleep is fitful with nightmares.

ORACLE:
Say no more! No need for you to worry
The keeper of Dzimbahwe is alive,
He will come back beyond this mist.
And you, isn`t it white hair I see there?
Have you no wisdom to show little boys the way of your fathers?
Can a chick, even a clever one, crow on the day it is hatched?

OLDMAN:

Speak softly Grandfather of the nation,
We teach them very well but we seem to fail.
Your little ones now walk with their feet in the air
They now think it is us the elders who must clap hands to them.

ORACLE:
I who speaks am Chaminuka himself.
Nothing I have seen this year makes me happy,
Nothing at all, not even one thing.
But if you people should torment my wrath
Behold I will descend on you in streaks of fire
That can slash a man into two! (*he roars terrifyingly*)

OLDMAN:
Speak gently to children, O Great Spirit,
For when you talk Mosiyatunya is but a whisper.
Speak softly, Sower of shooting stars,
Taura nehunyoro, Mudzimu Mukuru. (*He claps hands*)

ORACLE:
The time to reckon to your graves is nigh,
Everyone will soon know who I am.
I am the voice that speaks in the wind;
The bateleur spirit that rides on clouds
Watching all the mischiefs of Earthlings from up high.
Cursed be Hunter! *Cursed* be Farmer!
You just wait and see- just wait and see,
I will suck their blood with lice big as hyenas.
Namai'angu Shiri, vacharira nemuhapwa segurwe.

OLDWOMAN:
(*Ululates*) Shine your sun Nyaminyami,
You who wed The Zambezi with a yearlong rainbow.
Open our eyes that we may see between our princely twins
Who the bed-wetter is and who the best-man be.

ORACLE:
Nhai imi makarerwa neuchi,
Ishurai kwamuri gore rinofa nyuchi nenzara?

OLDMAN:
(*Clapping hands*) We are but little children;
O Healer of my people, we can't read your riddles

ORACLE:
That man you killed. That man and all others murdered.
Your fore-fathers are sneezing with the reek of innocent blood
More trouble is on the way until his spirit lies down.
And, as if that is not an abomination enough,
I see uninitiated feet muddling the Tower of Dzimbahwe.
(*makes the terrifying roars again*)

OLDMAN:
Ipwere dzemusha wako Chaminuka woye;
Forgive your children, Mudzimu *Mukuru*,
Like little chicks they can't tell between a fire and a flower.
What shall we do, O Great-One,
That our land may be freed from this terror?

ORACLE:
When the foolish ones see the wilderness
They think it's a city,
But their folly will not go unpunished.
Go home hoary-ones,
The gods do not need a mortal to fight their wars
Nor the mouths of the living to plead their cause.
But that river of blood must be stopped
And the spirits of those needlessly slain
You must pacify, I think you know how.
Go home now, and don't look back.
(Oldman and Oldwoman clap hands then exit)

ON THE ROAD THAT LEADS BACK TO THE VILLAGE

OLDWOMAN:
I wish Old Chibwe could be found
To hear for himself those words of Chaminuka.

OLDMAN:
No need to worry,
he'll come back 'beyond this mist' as the oracle said
Once more The Tower shows it is greater than all of us
Let alone those little boys who arrived on Earth this morning.
We should tell someone though, what the oracle said.
Who then shall we tell?

OLDWOMAN:

Neither Hunter and definitely not Farmer
Those two survive on instinct and not on sense.
You know, you can substitute the word *politician*
With *wild-animal* and never lose any meaning.

ENTER MAZWI THE POET WITH A RADIO. WITHOUT TALKING TO THE TWO HE SITS ON A PIECE OF ROCK AND TURNS UP THE VOLUME ON THE RADIO.

RADIO:
Here`s the news read by Lieton Manyepo.
Prince Farmer has formed a new political party.
Retired soldier CoNFuSD Buffalo,
Former police Chief Commissioner Beres Hyena
And the Squadron Commander Hippo Thomas have joined him.
But news we have just received says Hunter has formed another outfit
The business mogul Elephant, together with his arch enemy Professor Lion Shumba, among others have thrown their weight behind him.
Now when these two troops meet there is so much clawing   caterwauling, stampeding, mudslinging and bull-dust...

OLDWOMAN:
What kind of animal is a politician?
Wau, if they ask you this question on the twenty-seventh
I bet you know what not to say.
EXEUNT ALL

ACT 5: SCENE 1

IT IS 27 JUNE, VOTING DAY. IN THE VOTING HALL THE VOTERS ARE STANDING IN A LONG QUEUE WAITING TO MAKE THEIR CHOICE.

NARRATOR:
Following the murdering of the teacher and the disappearing of the King, the nation is cursed. The people are plagued with weak eyes and slow minds. Although the ballots have the names and insignia of Hunter and Farmer no-one can read them. So two boxes are provided and voters are asked to stand in two queues one for Hunter and the other for Farmer. Farmer and Hunter are called to stand each by his own box to enable the people to choose. The two have come wearing identical clothes, spotting similar beard and hair styles, and this has created a new problem.

OLDWOMAN:
(Aside) They said Farmer is the one to my left,
Now which one is my left hand?
Is my right hand on the left?

OLDMAN:
(Aside) They say Hunter is the one who smiles the most,
Now both of them are smiling.

PREACHER:
(Aside) I still haven`t seen between horn and fifteen Billion
I think I shall go for the billions.
No, with fifteen billion I can't buy even a bun.

Let me bless the horned one with my *X*!
Now, which one is Farmer? Hunter?
They look equally angry to me.
Let me go out and think first *(he exits).*

HUNTER:

(To himself) My line is longer but Farmer's line is not shorter.

FARMER:

(To himself) Hunter's queue is shorter but mine is not longer.
What can I do? *Right*, if I stand between the boxes, in addition to my supporters I might also confuse Hunter's followers into voting for me.
(He *moves to the centre, but Hunter makes the same move. They collide and become mixed up)*

1st TWIN:

What are you doing in my place?
Go back to your side.

2ND TWIN:

This is my place! You start it again,
That's what you always do
When you have wetted your side of the bed!

1ST TWIN:

Who wets the bed, you thief!
You steal my lunch every day, now you want to steal my name!

2ND TWIN:
That's nonsense, you crazy betrayer!
If you are not Hunter
How can I be him or Farmer or not?
THE TWINS START SHOUTING ANGRILY, NUDGING
AND SHOVING VIOLENTLY AT EACH OTHER. VOTING
STOPS. FOR SOME TIME, THE PEOPLE DO NOT KNOW
WHAT TO DO.

OLDWOMAN:
(*Asking the people*) Now what shall we do,
These two boys do not know who is not the other?
It's only the King who can tell them apart,
Yet no-one knows where he is. Can't we…?

SOLDIER:
Take a break for snuff, Old Bag.
(*To the people*) We will now use the secret-ballot,
Which means you must never know who you are voting for.
Everyone shall vote blind folded.
Cast your votes in the box that's left on the right.
You might be coming from the left or from the right
Or from nowhere; use the box that is right to the left.
Do so now!

OLDMAN:
My son, we do not understand…

SOLDIER:

Therefore, you are the right voters
For this kind of election.
So start voting. No more talking!

MAZWI SNEAKS IN, HIS HAND IS STILL IN BANDAGES.

MAZWI:
This election is a dereliction,
In this kind of election
Ballot rhymes with bullet
And both rhyme with *bullshit*.

SOME PEOPLE BREAK DOWN LAUGHING

SOLDIER:
You have picked the wrong joke
From the waste-paper-basket of your head.
You talk again you *die*!

THE PEOPLE VOTE QUIETLY. AFTER A WHILE IT'S TIME TO ANNOUNCE THE RESULTS.

SOLDIER:
The results! Yeah, yeah, listen to the results.
Our results are 51 to 49
But we don`t know as yet who got 49.

THE PEOPLE START TO COMPLAIN AND TO LEAVE.

1ˢᵀ TWIN:
Ladies and gentlemen, thank you very much for choosing me, we look forward to working tog…

2ᴺᴰ TWIN:
The madness in your head is getting worse,
How can 49 be the winner?
(*To the people*) my honorable people,
I`m happy that you have seen the wisdom of electing me,
I promi…

1ˢᵀ TWIN:
My good people do not listen to this shameless fraudster
He is not Hunter and I`m not Farmer
Actually he is not himself and myself I am.
See he is a bit taller than me, come measure us!

2ᴺᴰ TWIN:
No, you are not Hunter and I am not Farmer
In fact you are not and I am not who you say I am!

OLDWOMAN:
Someone please find a measure for this troublesome pair
Who claim to have seen the shadow of sound!

SOLDIER:
I will measure them both.
Stand back you! And hold your straying tongues.
Stand straight while I measure you!

Good. Right, umm yes.
Yes the results! Hear the results…

PEOPLE:
Yes, we would like to hear the results!

SOLDIER:
Twin to my left, two milligrams short……

PEOPLE:
Hua-a-a! Nonsense! You used the wrong tool
You can't hike the Inyanga in a canoe!
Or hunt sea-lions in a game reserve!
Yea, yea, give him one-decade time off to wash his bandolier!
MORE PEOPLE LEAVE IN DISAPPOINTMENT

MAZWI:
(To the people) Alright, alright, calm down;
We have seen enough nonsense in one afternoon
To last us a century *(some people listen)*.
To Prince Hunter and Prince Farmer,
It should be understandable to every smoker
If the match misses the fag and lights the beard.
Youth is bestowed with all the innocence
But age is blessed with all the experience…

1ST TWIN:
You left me right here, now you are right where you left me …

2ᴺᴰ TWIN:
I'm not standing on your left;
How many left hands do you have?

THE TWINS START WRESTLING EACH OTHER FIERCELY. AFTER A COUPLE OF MINUTES, THEY CHASE ONE AFTER THE OTHER OUT OF THE VOTING HALL. STILL RANTING AND FUMING THEY RACE EACH OTHER TOWARDS THE HORIZON AND DISAPPEAR INTO THE MOUNTAINS. THE PEOPLE ARE STUPEFIED; THEY DO NOT KNOW WHAT TO DO. GENERALLY, THERE IS A FEAR AMONG THE ELDERLY AND ANGER AMONG THE YOUTHS.

MAZWI:
Paradise lost! Paradise lost! *(The people listen)*
Yes, paradise can be lost
And a people lost with it
But out of soapstone, shall fly again
The black phoenix,
The unkillable totem of Zimbabwe!
But people, listen a little to what *Ambuya* has to say!

OLDWOMAN:
[*Rising*] Wau, give me your snuff bottle first.
Inzwai imi nyenye dzeZimbabwe,
Mucharamba muchizunguniswa senyenyedzi dzemudziva
Dzinobonderaniswa nekushambira kwegwavava
Kusvikira moziva kuti mutambo wekutonga

Haupfekerwe shangu dzineminzwa senhabvu.
Saka imi mose munoda kuba nyika
Kana kuiita musengabere
Dzokeraizve kune madzisekuru enyu mudzidziswe tsika
Nekuti mucharohwa nechamusingaone semheni.
To begin with, bow down your heads and let us pray.

_____END_____

AFRICA

We must now be born again in our blackness
To cast off our old black skin
And take on a new unkillable black personality
Or else Africa's tears
Will continue to burn down the old wine skins.

We must now arise from the centuries old death
And shove with one momentous heave
At the huge tombstone that's blocking our resurrection
Or else the remnant of our sanity
Will be smothered under the windswept sand dunes
Of an ideological Sahara
Or else Africa's unborn

Will forever be crucified by an ugly history.

We must delve deep
Deep into the darkest depths of our black souls
To salvage the black sunlight from siltation
And allow its shining imagination to blossom
Or else Africa's creative genius
Emaciated by many decades of self-denial
Will shrivel with the hand holding a begging bowl
To meet its death queuing for a food hand out…

Mmap Fiction and Drama Series

If you have enjoyed *The Twins*, consider these other fine books in **Mmap Fiction and Drama Series** from *Mwanaka Media and Publishing*:

The Water Cycle by Andrew Nyongesa
A Conversation…, A Contact by Tendai Rinos Mwanaka
A Dark Energy by Tendai Rinos Mwanaka
Keys in the River: New and Collected Stories by Tendai Rinos Mwanaka
How The Twins Grew Up/Makurire Akaita Mapatya by Milutin Djurickovic and Tendai Rinos Mwanaka
White Man Walking by John Eppel
The Big Noise and Other Noises by Christopher Kudyahakudadirwe
Tiny Human Protection Agency by Megan Landman
Ashes by Ken Weene and Umar O. Abdul
Notes From A Modern Chimurenga: Collected Struggle Stories by Tendai Rinos Mwanaka
Another Chance by Chinweike Ofodile
Pano Chalo/Frawn of the Great by Stephen Mpashi, translated by Austin Kaluba
Kumafulatsi by Wonder Guchu
The Policeman Also Dies and Other Plays by Solomon A. Awuzie
Fragmented Lives by Imali J Abala
In the Beyond by Talent Madhuku
Zororo Risina Zororo by Oscar Gwiriri
Sword of Vengeance by Olatubosun David
Finding A Way Home by Tendai Mwanaka
Your Epistle by Solomon A Awuzie

The Restless Run and Ruin of the Roaches and Rats by McLayode
The Reign of Terror by Ntando Gerald
Ibala Lyabwina Nama by Austin Kaluba
Daddy, Please Don't Kill Mama by Natisha Parsons
Pilate's Angels by Goodenough Mashego
Blue threads and other stories by Matthew Kunashe Chikono
The Sylvia Plath Effect by Shakemore Dirani

Soon to be released

https://facebook.com/MwanakaMediaAndPublishing/

www.ingramcontent.com/pod-product-compliance
Lightning Source LLC
Chambersburg PA
CBHW070848160426
43192CB00012B/2360